IND

1. WHAT IS ISO?

International organization for standardization (ISO) introduced ISO 14001Environment management system in 1992 and now in its fourth edition it is ISO 14001:2015.

Standard is based on the following premises:

1. Generic standard- applicable to every organization (Manufacturing/ service, Small /Large)
2. Plan-Do-Check-Act (PDCA)
3. Process approach- applicable to all organizational activities
4. Risk based approach- Management of uncertainties
5. Continual improvement- stepwise small improvements
6. Goal of sustainable development.
7. Involving all functions of the organisation

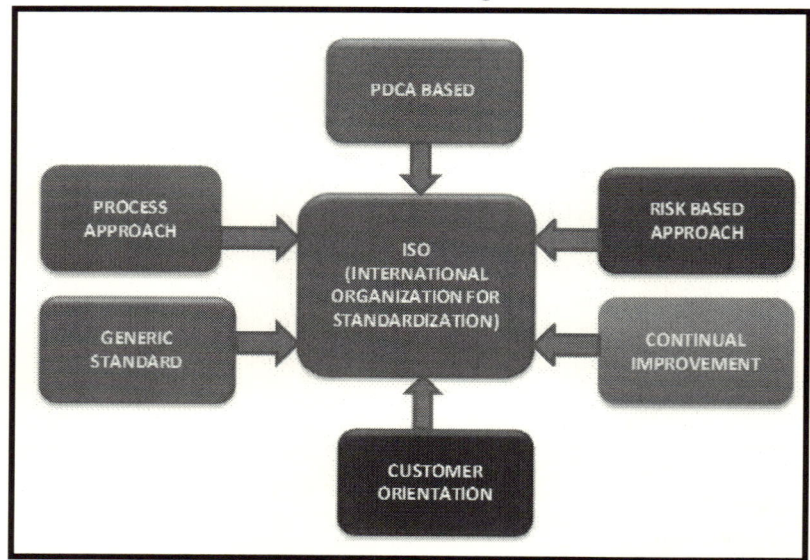

Characteristic features of ISO 14001 standard

2. ISO 14001TIMELINE

ISO 14001 has been changed as follows:

1. First edition: ISO 14001:1992
2. First revision ISO 14001:1996
3. Second revision: ISO 14001:2004

4.   Third revision: ISO 14001:2015

3.   ISO 14001 IMPLEMENTATION BENEFITS

- Encourages proactive and participative approach for improving environmental performance
- Enables development of structured processes for sustainable development
- Mitigates and controls the risk of adverse effects on environmental performance
- Meets the needs and expectations of interested parties related to environment
- Achieves the intended outcomes of the organization for environmental performance.
- Ensures the long term competitiveness and sustainability of the organization.
- Facilitates continual improvement in environmental performance through leadership accountability.

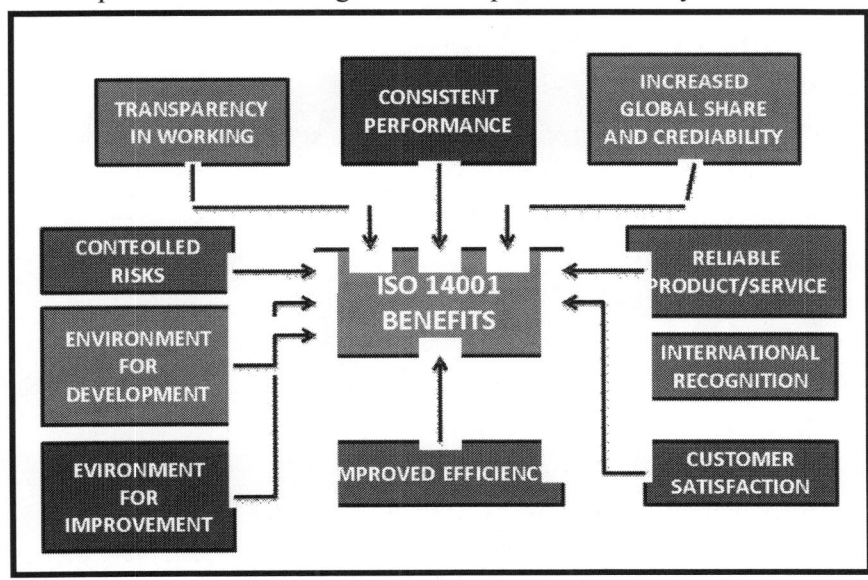

Benefits of ISO 14001

4. PRINCIPLES OF ENVIRONMENT MANAGEMENT

Seven management principles:

1. Interested Party focus- Fulfilling interested party requirements to enhance satisfaction for environment protection, waste management and sustainable development.
2. Leadership– Commitment , direction, accountability, resources provision & review of EMS
3. Engagement of people– Ownership and participation in environmental performance improvement
4. Process approach– Sequence, acceptance criterion & its monitoring and measurement of EMS
5. Improvement – Review , analysis and corrective- preventive actions for environment projects
6. Evidence-based decision making: Factual data based actions related to environmental performance and intended outcome
7. Relationship management- Relationship with interested parties through identifying the relevant needs and expectations.

5. WHAT IS ISO 14001:2015?

ISO 14001-2015 is Environment management System standard which is based on the following:
- Risk based thinking
- PDCA cycle
- Process approach
- 10 Clauses
  - 1. Scope
  - 2. Normative Reference
  - 3. Terms & Definition
  - 4. Context of the organization
  - 5. Leadership
  - 6. Planning
  - 7. Support

- o   8. Operation
- o   9. Performance evaluation
- o   10. Improvement
- ➢   Improvement focus
- ➢   Leadership accountability
- ➢   Consideration of Internaland external contextual issues
- ➢   Focus on relevant interested parties, their needs and expectation.

6.   ISO 14001:2015 CERTIFICATION PROCESS

Processes for ISO 14001:2015 Certification:

1. Development, implementation and maintenance of ISO 14001:2015 requirements.
2. Conduction of internal audit and management review meeting.
3. Application for certification to certification agency.
4. Receiving the quotation and placing the order.
5. Stage I audit.
6. Compliance to stage I audit findings.
7. Stage II audit.
8. Compliance to stage II audit findings.
9. Receipt of certificate.

7.   CONTEXT OF ORGANIZATION (4.1)

This is the new requirement of the standard which requires the organisation to identify and analyse the contextual issues relevant to the EMS of the organisation.

- ➢   Contextual issues- Factors and aspects affecting plan, process and working
- ➢   External issues: competitions, economic issues, environmental issues, social issues, political issues, legal

requirements, regulatory and technological changes, practices and plans at domestic as well as global level.

➢ Internal issues: culture, beliefs, values, or principles within the organization

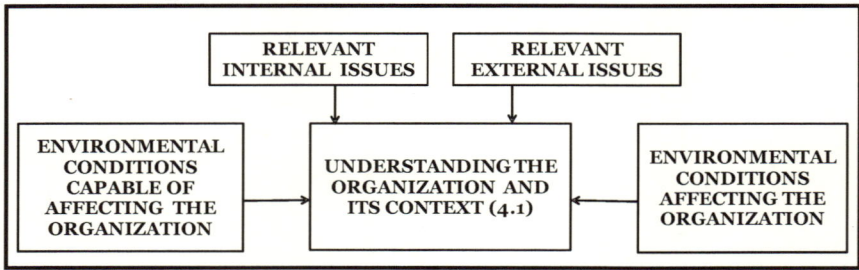

Understanding the organisation and its context

8. EXTERNAL ISSUES: SOURCES

1. Reports relating to global conditions, economic environment, technological reports, Interested parties feedbacks, complaints and expectations.
2. Reports relating to supplier and vendor, political stability and changes, investment opportunities, social factors, new laws and acts, changes in policies and regulations.
3. Reports related to changes in legislation and regulation related to environment as well as labour laws.
4. Feedbacks related to product/service performance and lessons learned.
5. Risk analysis and environmental audit reports.

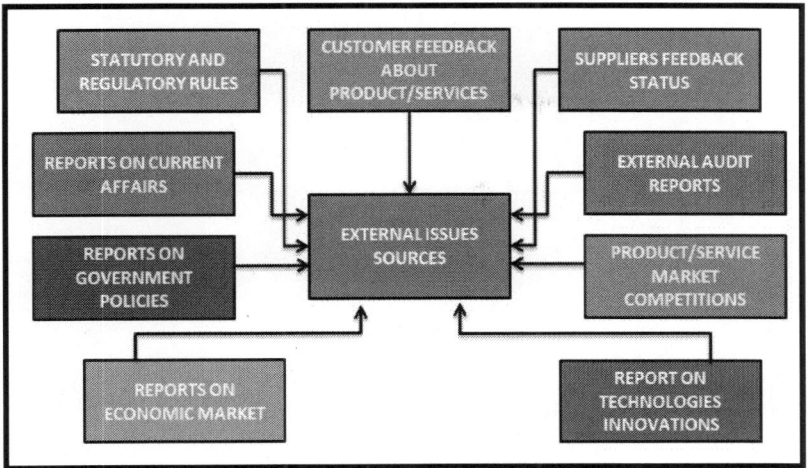

Sources of external issues

9.   INTERNAL ISSUES: SOURCES

1.   Organizational structure, including roles, responsibilities and governance arrangements;

2.   External reports showing how well the organization is performing for sustainable development;

3.   Mission, vision and core values of organisation;

4.   Business ethics, organizational codes of conduct and their importance;

5.   Feedback obtained from interested parties;

6.   Information management systems

7.   Organizational environmental capability studies

8.   Environment risk management plan.

9.   Availability of reliable, qualified and competent workforce for EMS – HR report.

10.   External provider's competence and availability to comply with requirements of EMS.

11.   Internal culture, values, politics, conflicts.

12.   Root cause analysis implementation, improvement tools and abilities to apply.

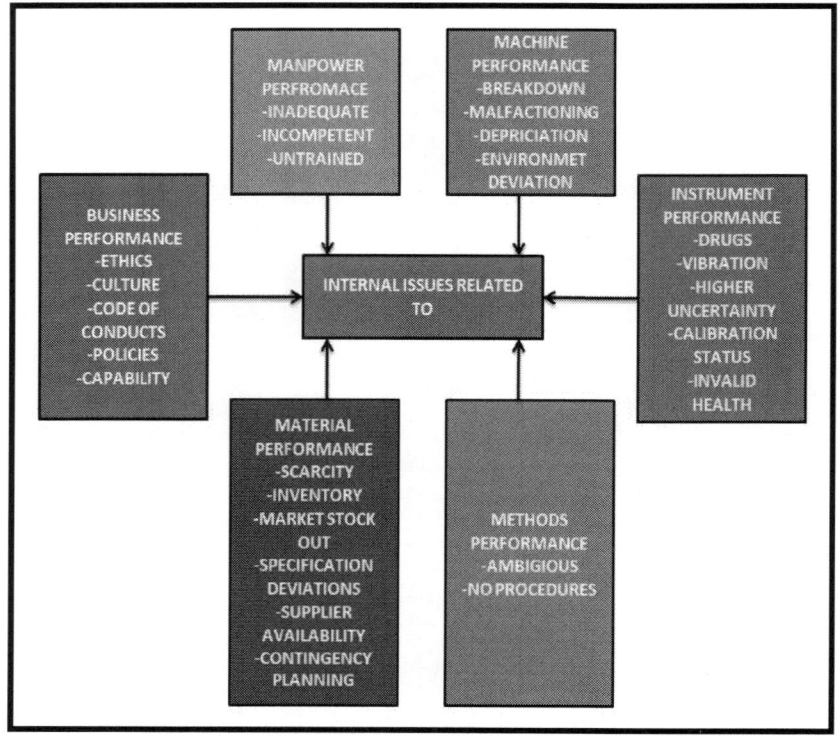

Sources of internal issues

10. INTERESTED PARTIES (4.2)

This is a new requirement of the standard and requires organisation to identify the relevant interested parties related to EMS and also the relevant needs and expectations.

Interested party- Those interested and/or affected by decision or activity of organization.

External interested parties-Customers, Suppliers, legal bodies, society.

Internal interested parties-owners, management and staff (permanent and temporary).

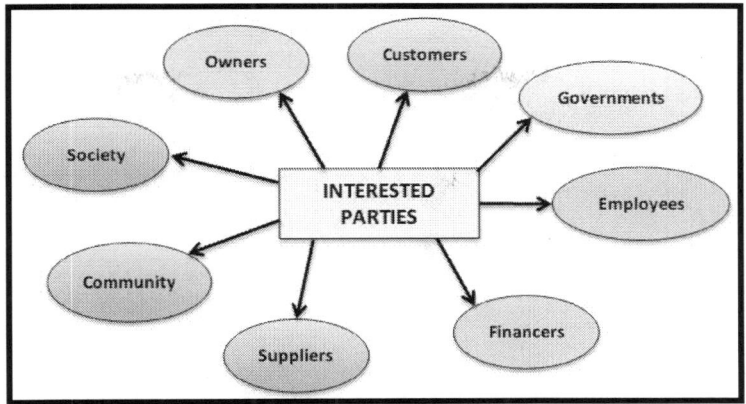

Stakeholders/interested parties

11. COLLECTING REQUIREMENTS OF INTERESTED PARTIES

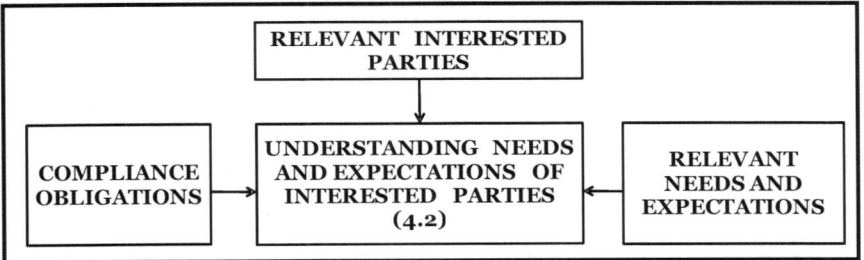

Capturing the Requirements of interested parties

12. SCOPE OF EMS (4.3)

Scope of registration/certification should clearly define:

1.   Scope of the EMS : Processes/departments/function covered
2.   Organization's main processes for its product/service delivery activities
3.   ISO 14001:2015 clause /sub clause exclusion
4.   Constraints or boundaries or limitations

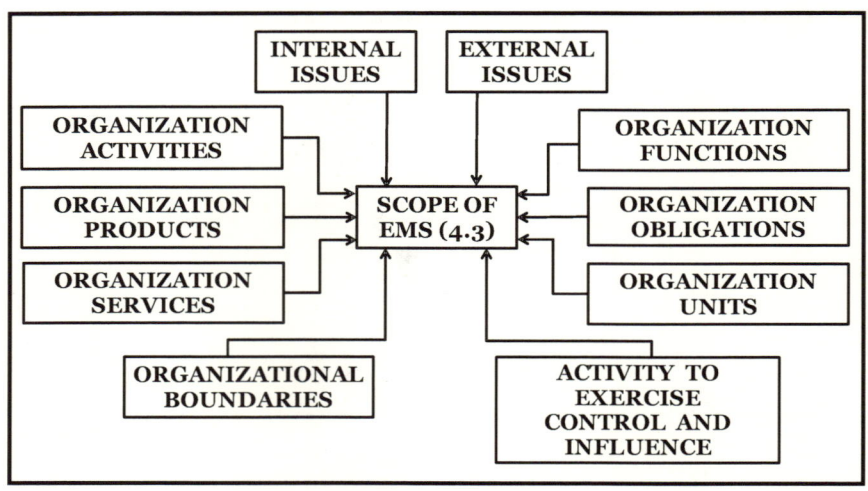

Scope of EMS

13. EMS AND ITS PROCESSES (4.4)

ISO 14001-2015 is based on process approach. It requires the organisation to identify the processes, interlink them, decide the intended outcomes of the process, set environmental objectives and targets, identify the risks and opportunities and plan for the improvement of the process.

Process: Input -Process-Output- Feedback

Step I: Identify key processes, support processes and sub-processes

Step-II: Draw the process flow

Step-III: Identify the process interface/interactions

Step IV: Identify critical/major points in the process

Step- V: Decide the acceptance criteria and monitoring and measuring mechanism

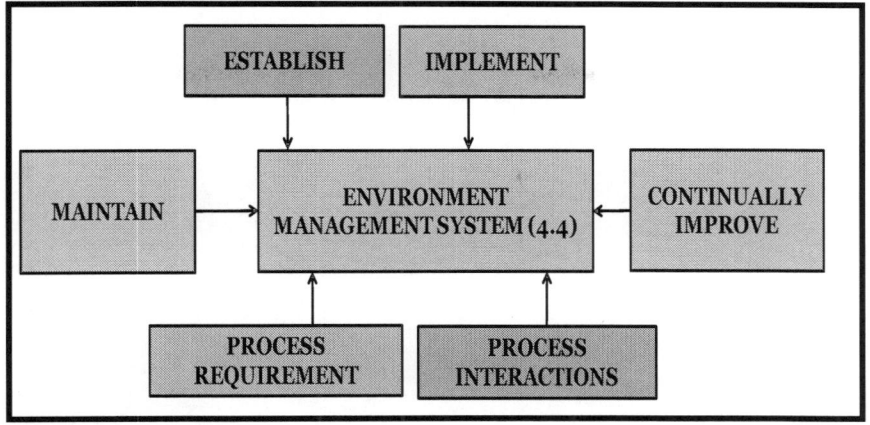

EMS and its processes

14. LEADERSHIP (5.0)

The ISO 14001-2015 gives importance to the Leadership and requires it to shoulder the accountability for the EMS>
Leadership responsibility:

- Express commitment for EMS
- Setting of policies and objectives.
- Planning
- Responsibility and authority delegation
- Risk and opportunity analysis and management
- Provision of resources
- Internal and external communication.
- Creating an effective work environment.
- Reviews and improvements
- Statutory and regulatory compliance
- Creating the healthier environment to nourish ISO 14001:2015.

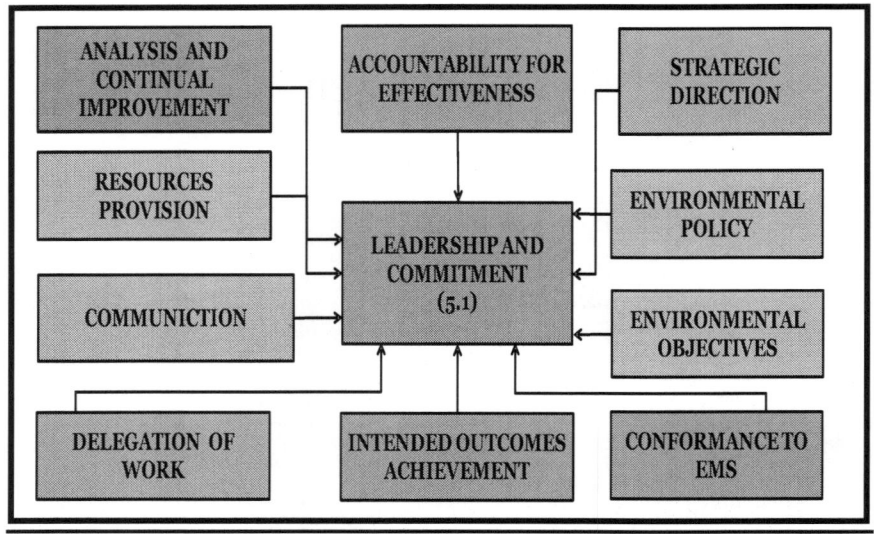

Leadership

15. ENVIRONMENT POLICY (5.2.1)

Policy: a direction given by top management to the organization.

➢ Simple, easily understandableand based on the organisations current focus.

➢ Communication to all employees

➢ Commitment to statutory and regulatory requirement

➢ Display at prominent locations.

➢ Available in local language.

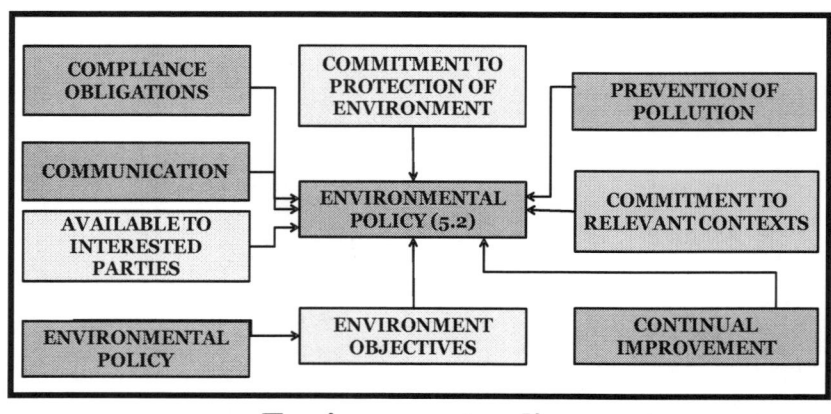

Environment policy

16. EXAMPLE: ENVIRONMENT POLICY

ENVIRONMENT POLICY

We are committed in protecting natural resources through continual improvement and execution of Environment Management system by-

- Establishing the objectives and target to improve environmental performance.
- Complying with all the applicable statutory & regulatory norms
- Using of 3R (Recycle, Reuse, Reduce) methodology for waste management
- Adopting sustainable development through environment friendly technology and system
- Building environmental awareness amongst the interested parties.

Date: 01.04.2019   **Director**

17. ORGANISATIONAL ROLES AND RESPONSIBILITIES (5.3)

Organization management-

➢ Organization structure, hierarchy and lines of reporting.
➢ Duties, responsibilities and authority of all personnel
➢ Communication to the concerned
➢ Avoids confusion and conflicts

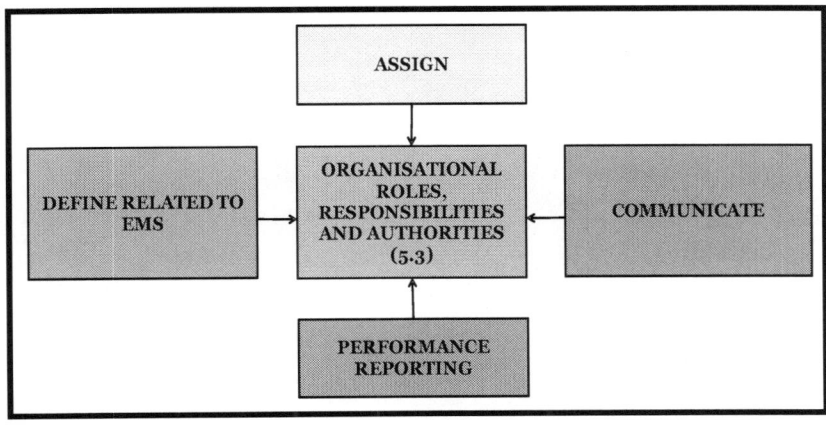

Roles, responsibility and authority

Responsibility of Environment Manager

- Implementing environmental policies, procedures and practices
- Develop management plan to meet targets and prepare performance reports
- Encourage the best practice in environmental conservation
- Establish systems to monitor performance and to implement strategies, management plan
- Ensuring compliance with applicable environmental statutory and regulatory requirements
- Analyze environmental performance data and reporting information to internal staff, clients and regulatory bodies
- Confirming that environment friendly procurement of materials, ingredients
- Management of environmental plan budgets
- Liaise with interested parties
- Leadership to identify, analyse& act on environmental issues within organisation
- Providing environmental training to staff at all levels and motivate them

18.   PLANNINGENVIRONMENT MANGEMENT SYSTEM (6.0)

Planning is the first step of plan-do-check-act and is important aspect of EMS.

Plan EMS to:

1. Promote a culture of risk-based thinking
2. Establish the methods to determine and address the risks and opportunities
3. Set the objectives: SMART
4. Determine products and services specifications
5. Promote improvement.

6. Provide framework for monitoring and measuring and gathering, analyzing and evaluating appropriate data and information.
7. Review and update.

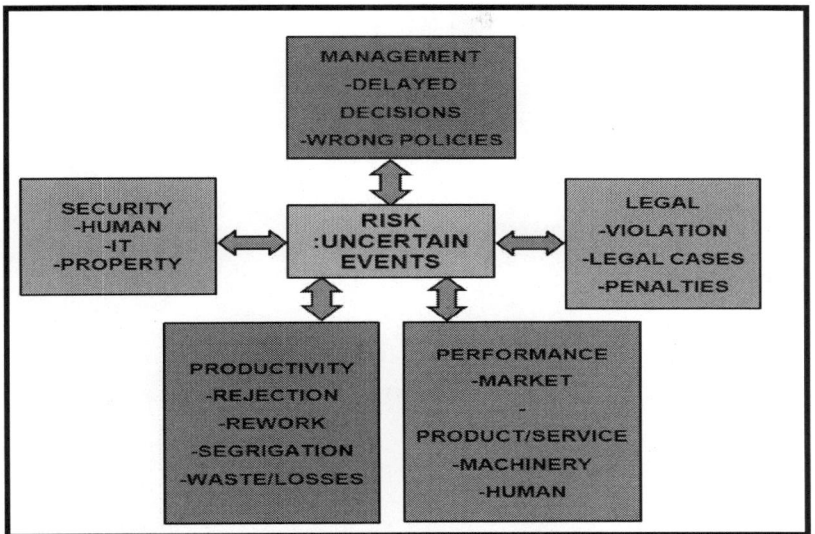

Risk Analysis

19. ADDRESSING THE RISK AND OPPORTUNITY (6.1)

Steps to address risk and opportunity:
1. Form the team.
2. Train the team
3. Study the organizational operations at each level
4. Identify the risk and opportunities
5. Establish the procedure for addressing the risk and opportunities
6. Follow the procedure
7. Brainstorm for prioritizing the risk and opportunity
8. Brainstorm the operational controls or improvement actions
9. Finalize the controls or improvement actions
10. Plan to execute the controls or improvement actions
11. Execute the controls or improvement actions

12. Evaluate the effectiveness of control or improvement actions by re-assessing the risk.

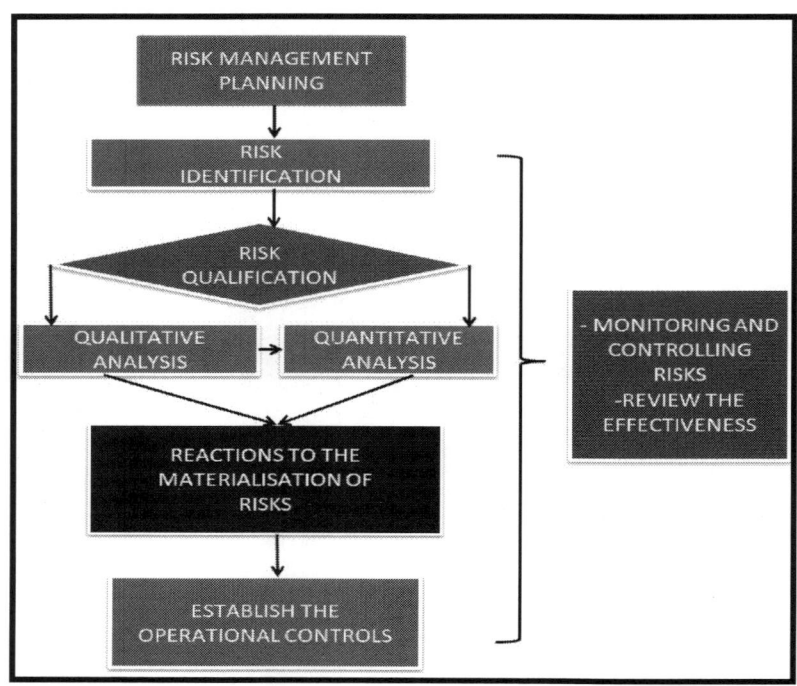

Addressing the risk and opportunity clause requirements

ASPECT-IMPACT ASSESSMENT

The environmental aspect is the element of an organization's activities or products or services that interacts or can interact with.

An environmental aspect can cause environmental impact(s). A significant environmental aspect is one that has or can have one or more significant environmental impact(s). The Environmental aspects are determined by the organization and impacts are monitored

Identification and updation of environmental aspects:

a. Aspect Identification and Impact Analysis is carried out once in a year.

b.	For this team of members headed by Environment Section Head is formed.

c.	This team reviews the incidents of past violations of environments, Environment audit reports, factory inspectors visit report etc., in order to find out area & situations affecting environment.

d.	In addition to this team takes round of different sections of the plant and notes down its observations relating to different aspects they came across.

e.	The team also interacts with the various personnel in the section to explore various situations in the section where environment is getting impacted.

f.	Reference check list is used by this team for identification of Aspects.

g.	Based on the aspects identified the team prepares report prioritizing the aspects as per the importance & also specifying the impact associated with it by brain storming.

h.	The actions which are required to be taken in current financial year are decided and initiated.

i.	The review of this is carried out during Management Review Meeting. Effectiveness of implementation is ensured.

j.	A comprehensive study of aspect identification is carried out once in 3 years. The report and actions are reviewed and implemented.

Significant Aspect & Controls Measures: Quantitative

S: Severity, S: Scale, O: Occurrence, D: Detection

RPN: Risk Priority number=S*S*P*D

Activity	Aspect	Impact	S	S	P	D	RPN	Signi ficat /Non- Signi fican	Control
Burning of Coal in Power plant	Release of Haz. Gases to air	Air Pollution	4	4	4	1	64	Signifi cant	Installing Absorbing filters to Chimney

Significant Aspect & Controls Measures: Qualitative

Sr.No.	Activity/Area affecting environment	Significant Environmental Threats (Aspects & its Impacts)	Precautionary Measure/Actions Planned
1	Maintenance/Servicing	Generation of waste like cotton waste, Rubber seals, metal parts, oils results in Land Pollution	Developing authorized Collection of waste mechanism Disposal of waste as per MPCB or applicable acts & Rules
2	Replacement of faulty parts, spares etc	Generation of waste result in land pollution.	Developing authorized Collection of waste mechanism Disposal of waste as per MPCB or applicable acts & Rules
3	Gas Welding , Cutting operations	Release of Fumes/gases results in air Pollution	Use of Standard work Practices like use of ISI mark regulation, Positioning of Gas Cylinders, Checking the safety valves etc.
4	Unloading of HCL acid from tanker to Bulk acid storage tank	Spillage of Acid on Land due to leakage may cause suffocation	Spraying water on Land Lime spread on spillage area
5	Filling of KOH solution in electrolysis module	Spillage of KOH Land due to leakage may result in skin contact	Wash infected area with Boric acid Wash with water
6	Ozone Dosing in drinking water	Release of Gas	Plant shall be isolated Attend Leaked valve
6	Curing of rubber lining with steam boiler	Generation of waste result in Land Pollution	Developing authorized Collection of waste mechanism Disposal of waste as per MPCB or applicable acts & Rules

20.   ENVIRONMENT OBJECTIVES (6.2)

Environment objectives: the statement of goal set related to business, product, service or process.

Aim of objective: to plan the actions and monitor and measure the achievements/performance.

Objectives are drafted in **SMART** way -

S- Specific means related to particular task, activity or intention.

M-Measurable should be expressed in terms of quantity

A-Achievable with present resources

R-Realisticto current issues and workload.

T- Time boundwith specific start and completion date.

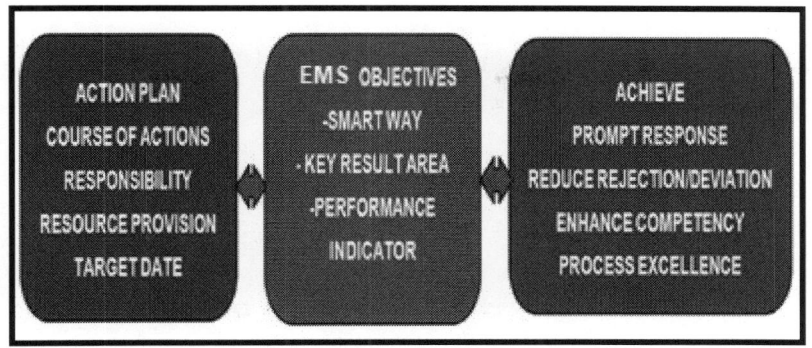

Environment objectives and plan

21. EXAMPLES OF SMART OBJECTIVES

1. To ensure 100% water recovery by March 2020.
2. To increase green belt area through plantation by 10% every ye March 2020ar.
3. To reduce carbon emission by 5% March 2020.
4. To reduce water consumption by 5% March 2020.
5. To reduce energy consumption by 5% March 2020.
6. To ensure application of 3R to waste generation .
7. To built up awareness amongst staff through trainings atleast 2 Mandays/year.
8. To increase environmental friendly procurement.
9. To comply 100% timely the applicable legal obligations.

22. OBJECTIVE: ACTION PLAN (6.2)

- Management actions,
- Resource requirement,
- Responsibility,
- Target date of accomplishment
- Structured way.

Precautions while preparing management program:
1) Avoid including the daily routine activities.
2) Include up-gradation of infrastructure, changes in existing process, adoption of new technology, improvement of skill, competency of people
3) Prepare stage wise anddetailed planto make monitoring easier.

23. FORMAT: MANAGEMENT PROGRAMME

1. Objective:
2. Performance criteria:
3. Present status:
4. Target:
5. Execution responsibility:
6. Action plan:

Sr. No.	Activity	Target date	Responsibility	Review/ Compliance status

7. Review frequency:
8. Benefits expected: Cost/Environment/environment/safety

PLAN OF CHANGES

A structured approach to managing changes includes:
- The consequences of the changes
- New risks and opportunities involved
- Notification to interested parties about the change.
- Availability of resources to implement the change
- Minimal disruption to the organization's operations.
  Changes may be due to:

- Statutory or regulatory requirements,
- Needs and expectations of interested,
- Competitions
- Other internal and external issues.

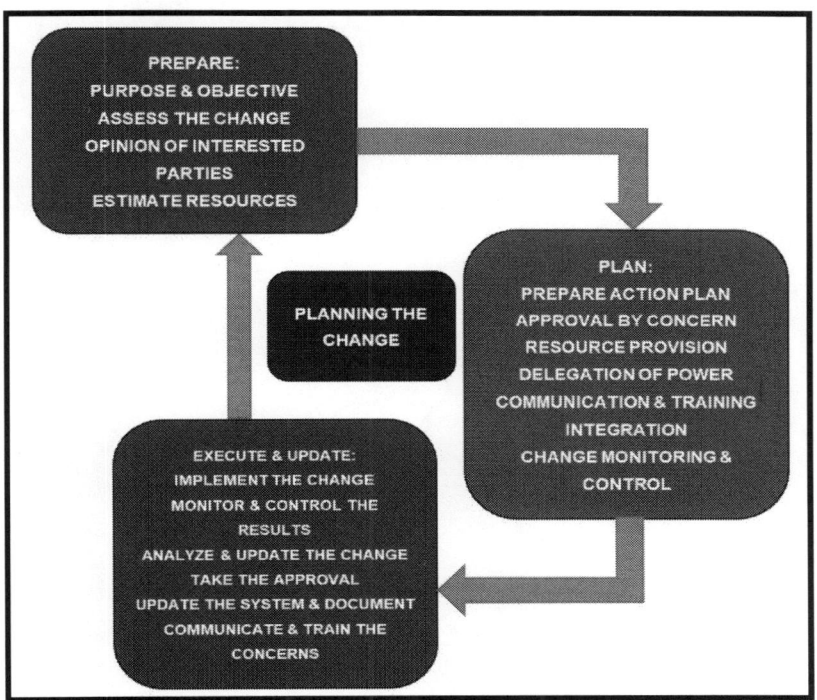

Plan of Changes

24. HUMAN RESOURCE DEVELOPMENT (7.1,7.2)

- Provide the manpower resources as per the job requirements.
- Prepare job profile for each job
- Allocate skilled, knowledgeable, and competent person for each job

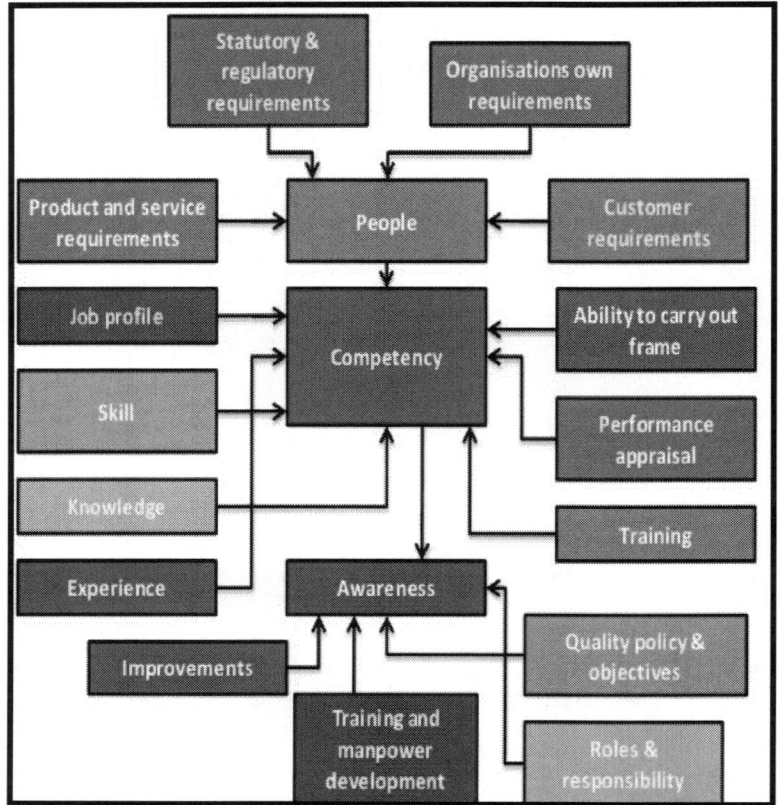

People, Competency and Awareness

25. AWARENESS &TRAINING (7.3)

- Create awareness about EMS, Policy, objectives, work process, job responsibilities
- Identify training needs
- Provide regular trainings
- Trainings can be on job, in-house or external

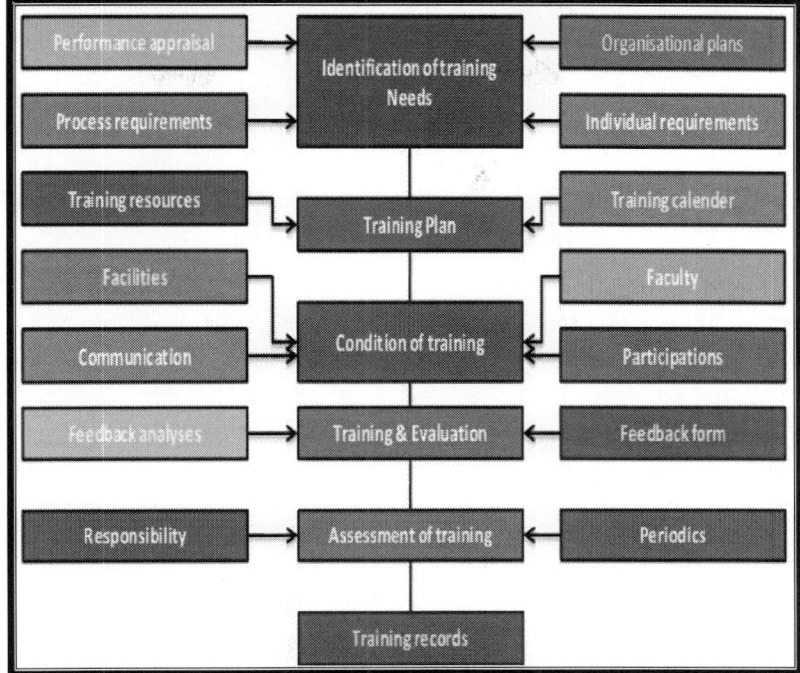

Training process

26. COMPETENCE (7.2)

- Competency is the ability to perform the job in successful way.
- Criteria for competency:education, skills, training and experience for activities, tasks, functions and processes.
- Various ways of building competency of manpower are through:
- Training,
- Changing processes,
- Improving procedures,
- Job rotation,
- Outsourcing the work,
- Role play,
- Recruiting fully trained and competent people.

ORGANIZATION KNOWLEDGE

Organization knowledge is knowledge which is specific to the organization and can be gained through experience, on job training and personal efforts.

Provide security and confidentiality about organizational knowledge.

Some of the ways to develop organizational knowledge are:

- Library.
- Conferences and seminars.
- E-portal, e- knowledge bank.
- Documentation, research journals.
- Interaction with other power plants on specific issue.
- Reports of failures and achievements.
- Project reports and learning.
- Visual displays.

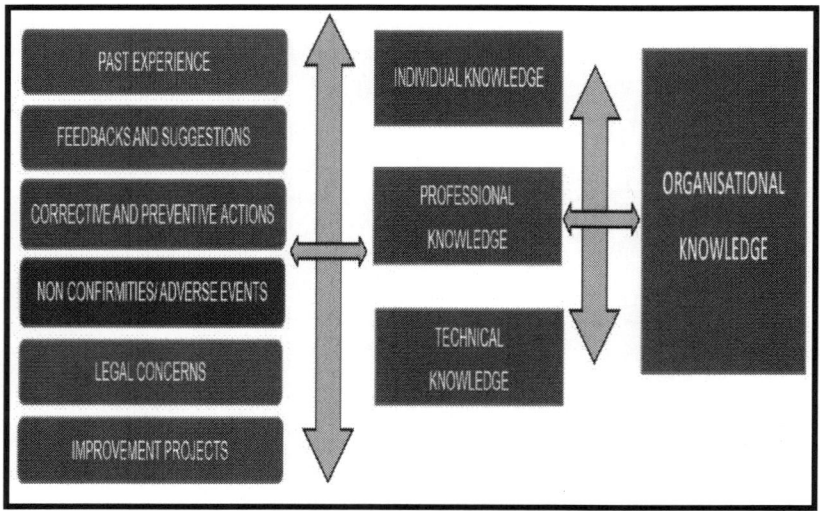

Organizational Knowledge

27. COMMUNICATION (7.4)

The organization can ensure the effective internal and external communications considering:

- What to communicate?
- When to communicate?
- With whom to communicate?

- How to communicate?

The various internal and external communications and the possible modes -

- Meetings
- Circular/notices/penalties/Advertisement
- Social media apps
- Complaints/feedbacks
- Phone/Mobile/video conferencing
- Training/Seminars/talks
- Visual management
- Audio video aids

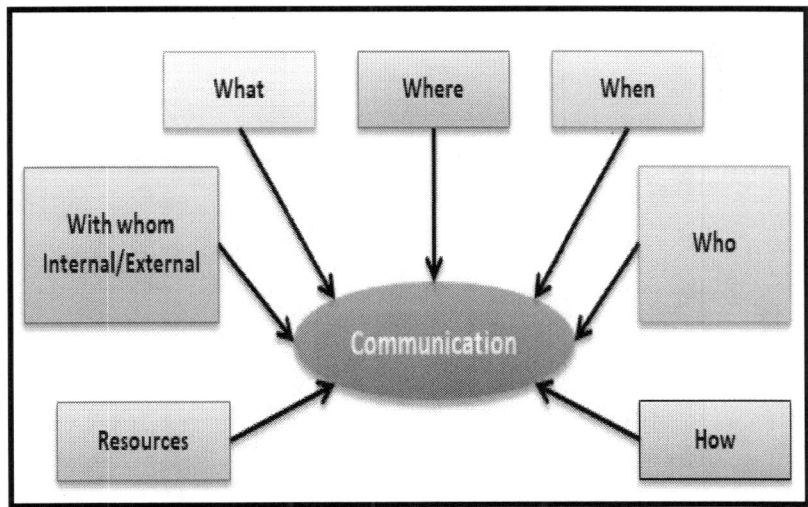

Communication

28. DOCUMENTED INFORMATION (7.5)

- Documented Information:data/information in any form which is utilized for further planning/analysis/decision making.
- Documented information control: document control and record control.
- Documented information type: soft or hard, paper, manuals/books, drawing, picture, Instructions, circulars, notes,

agreements, presentations, electronic software applications/programmes or photographs etc.

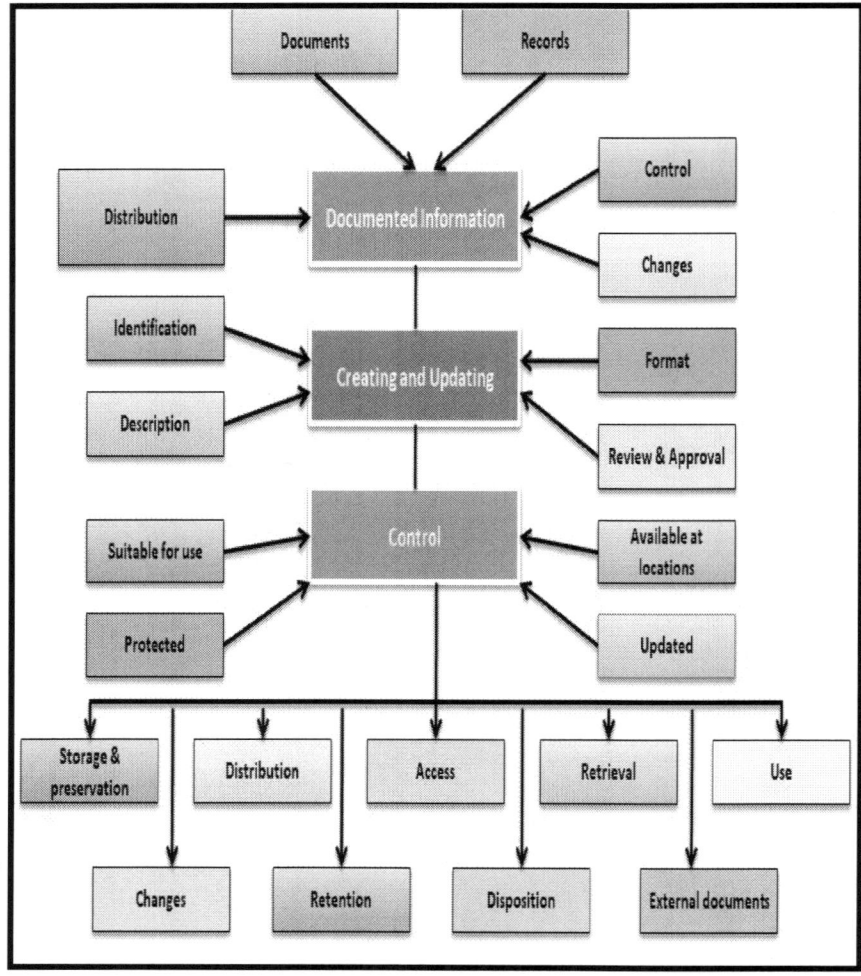

Documented Information

29. OPERATIONAL PLANNING AND CONTROL (8.1)

During the manufacturing of the products or providing services, the organization has to ensure:

- Process flow for each activity
- Key result areas/ critical control points for each process
- Proper identification and traceability,

- Preservation of products and services,
- Account for the changes,
- Specify the criteria and authority for release of products and services,
- Monitoring and measurement criterion by setting key performance indicators/objectives.
- Sequence of procedure/work Instruction, checklist wherever required
- Meet the requirements for post-delivery activities and
- Control the property belonging to customers or external providers.

Deviations from the specifications, criteria and documented processes have to be dealt with so that the customer gets the good Environment of products and services as per his requirement.

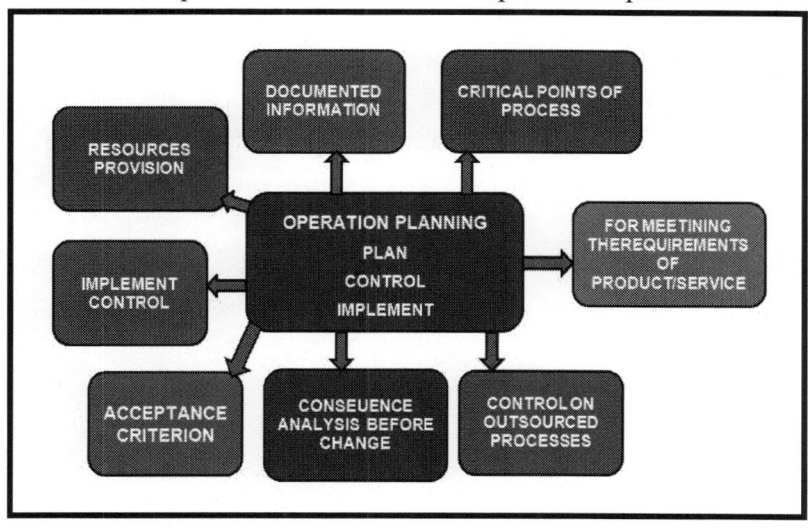

Operational planning and control

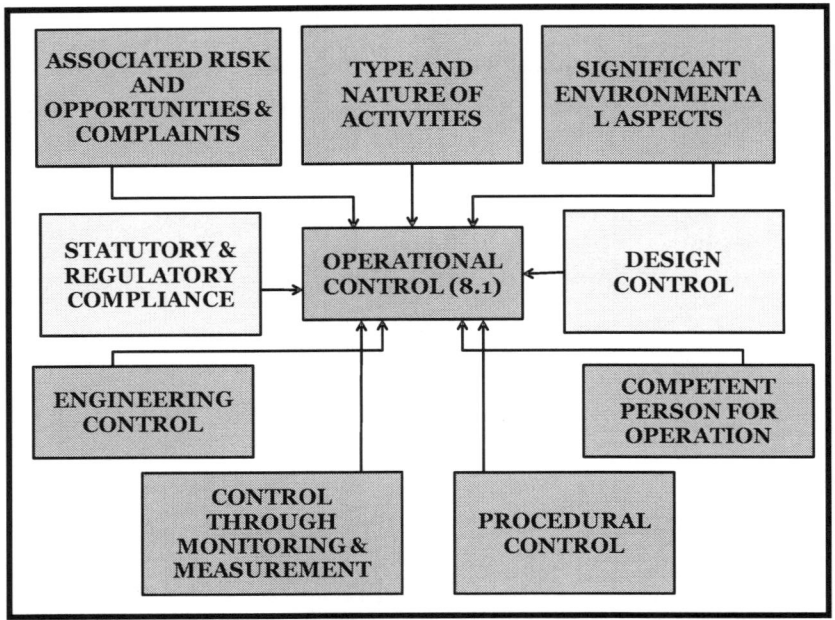

OUTLINE OF ENVIRONMENTAL MANAGEMENT PLAN

Organization has to commit for protection of environment through sustainable environment management plan and practices. For that the EMS objectives are:

1. Compliance with MOEF and other legally binding terms and conditions.

2. Ensure minimum impact on surrounding environment by project activities.

3. To implement measures for control of pollution.

4. To provide training on environment management and protection to all its employees and contract workers.

For this, organization has to carry out Environment risk analysis (Aspect-Impact Register), follow statutory and regulatory requirements and implements ISO 14001:2015 requirements.

A documented system consist of environment apex manual, environment procedures, environment standard operating procedure, legal register, Aspect Impact register, Emergency preparedness and rescue plan& forms and formats are developed for site specific work. This system will be implemented, maintained and monitored for effectiveness by taking appropriate corrective and preventive action. Environment Management System performance are reviewed and monitored against the set target and corrective action will be initiated.

Organization has to take all the applicable consent, implement it and monitor its performance. An onsite environment management cell is created for implementation, monitoring, liasioning, tracking and interacting with all the parties and stakeholders on environment issues. An organization structure with defined roles and responsibilities is prepared for the same with assigned authorities to stop the work in case of adverse situations.

Initial environment review and aspect impact analysis to be carried out for deciding the areas for improvement. Structured management program are created to ensure reduction of environment aspect/impacts.

Operational controls are to be put in place for reducing the environment aspect/impact.

Monthly environment audits needs to be carried out and internal and external audits of ISO 14001:2015are carried out. The performance and audit findings are reviewed by the management. During management review meetings and necessary resources are provided to ensure safe and risk free working environment to the site and surroundings. Management takes efforts for continual improvement of processes and enhance stakeholder satisfaction for sustainable development.

Regular monitoring of air, water, land, noise etc. will be carried out to assess the environment impacts.

Environment Emergency preparedness and rescue plan is prepared and operational controls are exercised effectively and monitored regularly.

Management has to commit for sustainable development in all its activities.

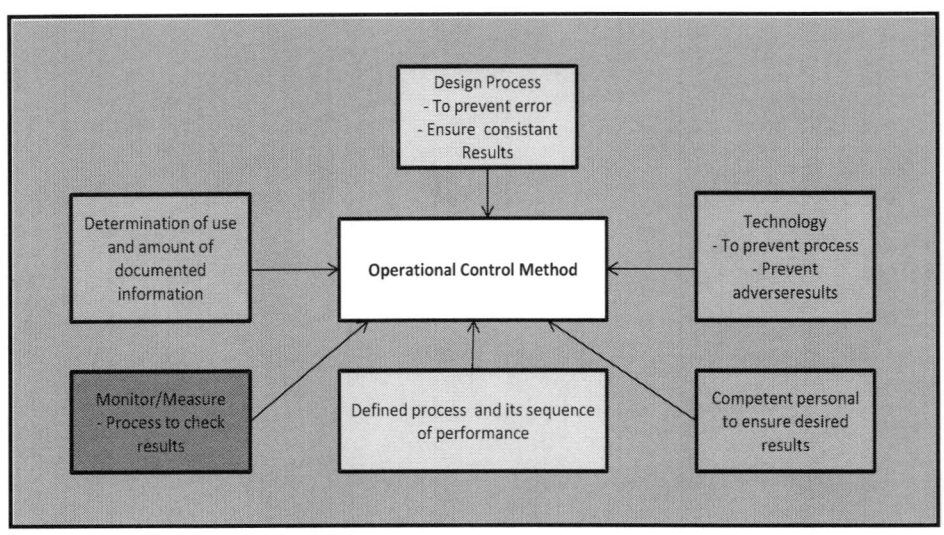

30. EMERGENCY PREPARDNESS & RESPONSE (8.2)

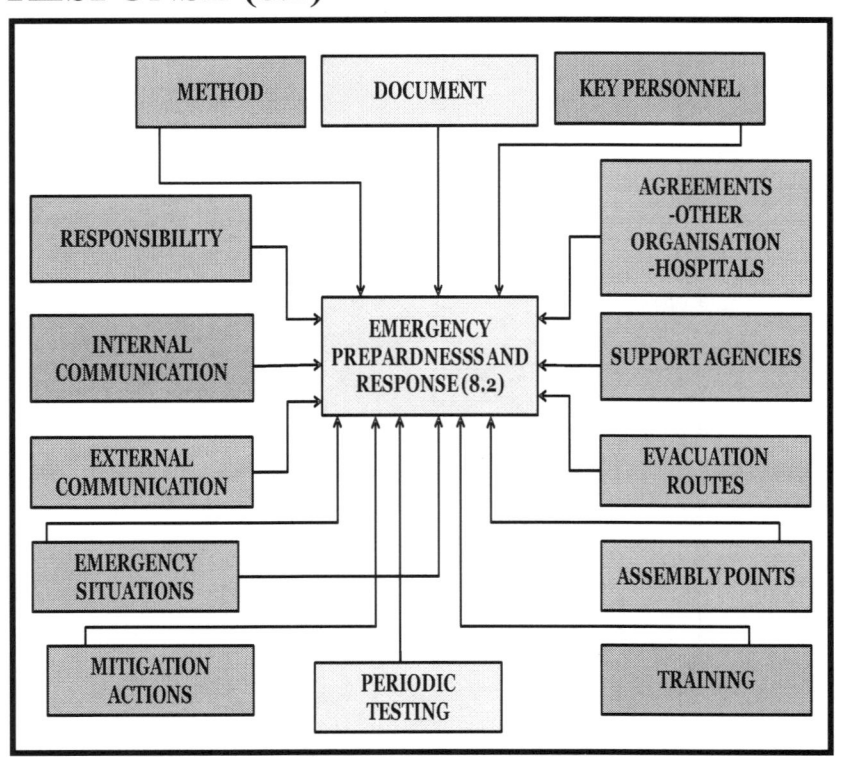

31. PERFORMANCE EVALUATION: MONITORING, MEASUREMENT, ANALYSIS AND EVALUATION (9.0)

A)   Measurement and monitoring:

☐   Monitor key characteristics of operations and processes that can have significant risk andits impacts and/or compliance consequences;

☐   Track performance and analyze trends;

☐   Calibrate and maintain measuring and monitoring equipment and

☐   Through internal audits, periodically evaluate compliance with requirements.

B) Customers' overall satisfaction, including:

►   Customer surveys.

►   Customer feedback on delivered products and services.

►   Meetings with the customer.

►   Market share analysis.

►   Compliments.

►   Warranty claims and dealer reports.

C) Monitoring and measurement help to:

☐   Evaluate performance;

☐   Analyze root causes of problems;

☐   Assess compliance with statutory and regulatory requirements;

☐   Identify areas requiring resources and corrective action,

☐   Improve performance and increase efficiency.

☐Make modifications through reviews

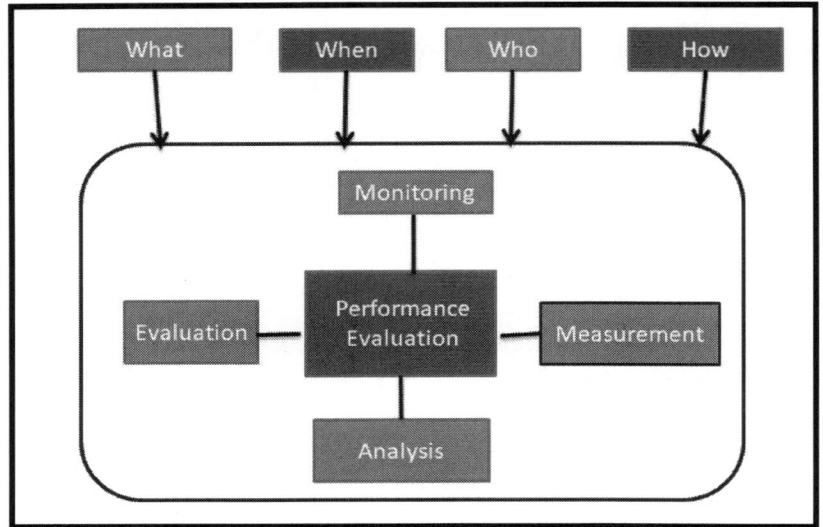

Performance evaluation

32.   PERFORMANCE EVALUATION (9.0)

1.   Decide what needs to be measured and monitored.

2.   Check if the acceptance criteria are specified, otherwise and establish the same.

3.   Explore the various methods of monitoring and measurement.

4.   Check if the concerned equipments and systems are available, tested and calibrated.

5.   Provide the responsibility.

6.   Prepare a measurement and monitoring program plan.

7.   Establish the data collection, analysis and reporting system.

8.   Take trials.

9.   Train the personnel and implement the system.

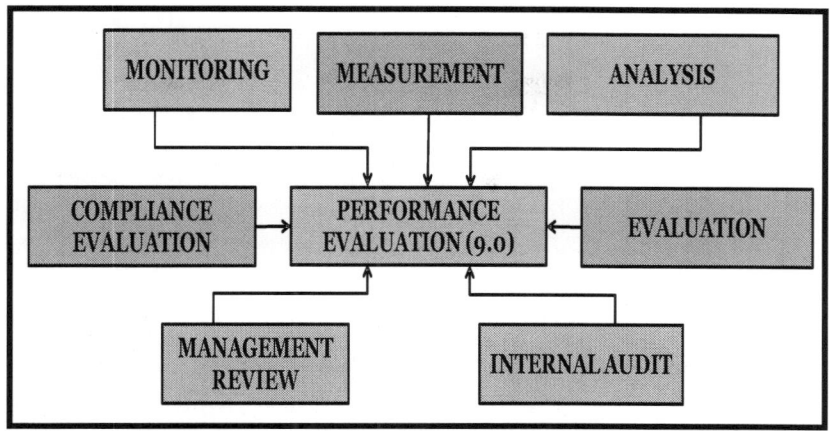

Elements of performance evaluation

33. MONITORING, MEASUREMENT & ANALYSIS

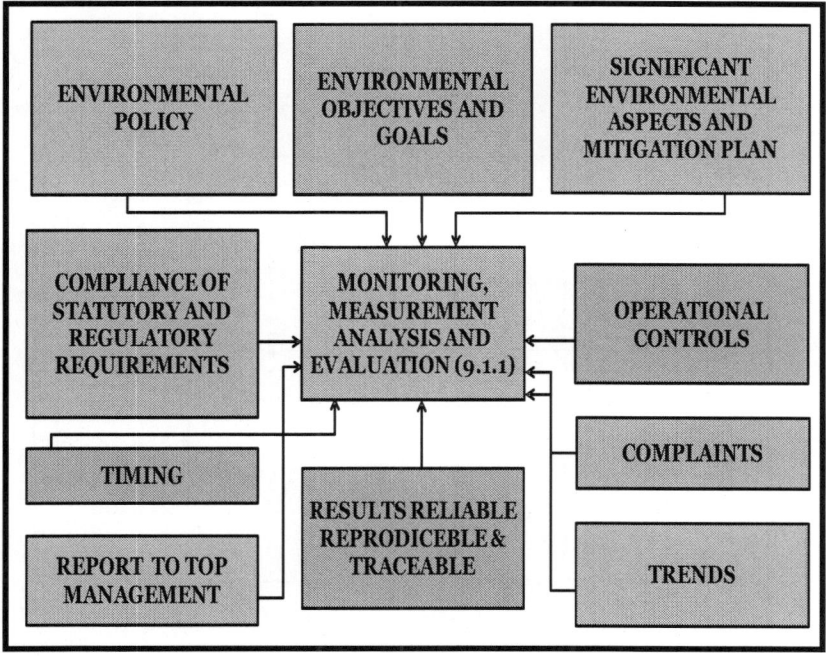

Example of Process Monitoring:

A.Waste Disposal

Input	Process	Output	Critical Control point	Process monitoring Point	Review Frequency	Record Ref
Waste, Chemical SOP	Landfill	Limits/criteria for acceptance of hazardous wastes for direct disposal to secured landfill	Bottom Liner- 1.300 mm Leachate Collection Layer 2.1.5mm HDPE 3. 450mm Blended Clay 4. Geotextile 5. 300 mm Drainage/Detection Layer 6. 1.5mm HDPE 7. 450mm Blended Clay Top Liner 1.300 mm Compacted Hard Murrum 2.750mm Blended Soil 3.1.5 mm HDPE 4.150mm Drainage Layer 5.750mm Yellow Soil 6.Vegetation	pH ,Heavy Metal,Sulphur etc.	During Each Landfill	Inspection Record

B. Environmental Activity: Process Monitoring

S. NO.	ACTIVITY	APR	MAY	JUN	JUL	AUG	SEP	OCT	NOV	DEC	JAN	FEB	MAR	RESP
1.	Submit environmental statement						☆							ABC
2.	Renewal of consent to operate		☆											ABC
3.	File water cess returns	☆	☆	☆	☆	☆	☆	☆	☆	☆	☆	☆	☆	ABC
4.	Testing of effluent	☆	☆	☆	☆	☆	☆	☆	☆	☆	☆	☆	☆	ABC
5.	Testing of stack emissions		☆						☆					PQR

34. COMPLIANCE OBLIGATIONS &EVALUATION COMPLIANCE (6.1.3,9.1.2)

Organization has to identify applicable legal and other requirements, its applicability to organization. Based on requirements organization should monitor, measure and evaluate the compliance. If compliances are deviating, organization should take the corrective measures.

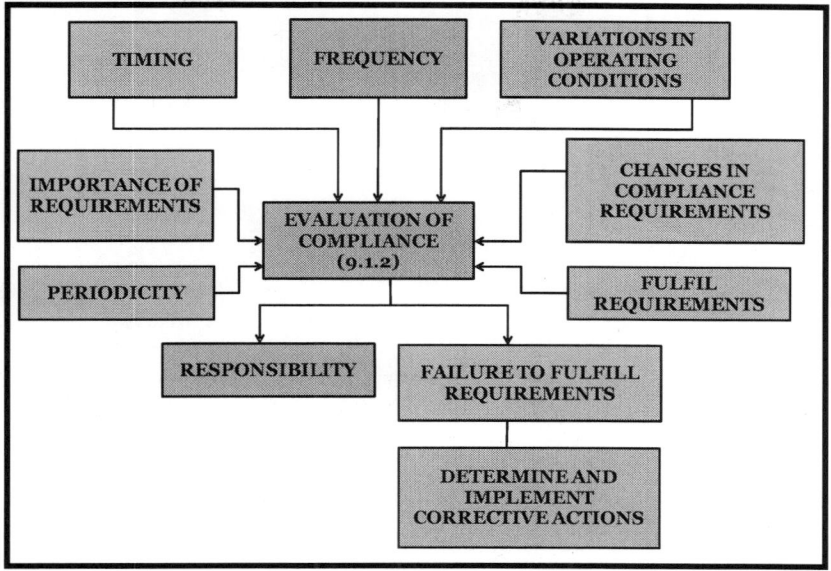

REGISTER OF LEGAL & OTHER REQUIREMENTS

Name of the act/rule	Latest Amend-ments	Aspects to be covered	Requirements	License /Consent No. & Date	Validity Period	Date of Renewal	Prescribed Limit	Responsible Department	Any Legal case or noncompliance	Measure to Control	Record Reference	Manual Reference
Under section 26 of the Water (Prevention & Control of Pollution) Act, 1974	Nil	Waste Water, Land degradation	Consent to establish and Consent to Operate	1234	-	2020	6000 MT/Yr	Commercial	Nil	Proper monitoring of parameters as per conditions specified under act	File 23	MPCB Manual & Resp. Act/Rule copy
Water Supply Regulations, 1973	Nil	Consumption of water	Payment of water charges	12345	Every month	Nil	Nil	Commercial	Nil	As per the regulations payments are made	File 23	
Minimum wages act, 1948	Nil	Wages as per requirement	Wages as per requirement	Nil	Nil	Nil	Wages as per requirement	Commercial	Nil	As per circular the payment are made	File 23	

EVALUATION COMPLIANCE RECORD

APPLICABLE ACT	Identification of legal requirement		Monitoring and measurement	Evaluation of compliance	Frequency
	Parameter	Allowable unit in mg/ltrs	Data of April- 2019		
	Industrial Effluent				
	pH	5.5 to 9.0	7.48	ok	
	Suspended Solids Max.	100	16	ok	
	BOD	30	18	ok	
	COD	250	67	ok	
	D.O.	>5	5.2	ok	
The water (prevention & control of pollution) act 1974	Oil and Grease Max.	10	<0.5	ok	Monthly
	Nickel	3	0.32	ok	
	Hexavalent Chromium	0.1	<0.05	ok	
	Zink	5	<0.05	ok	
	Total Chromium	2	<0.05	ok	
	Chlorides	600	57.57	ok	
	Domestic Effluent				
	Suspended Solids Max.	100	18	ok	
	pH	5.5 to 9.0	7.55	ok	Monthly
	BOD 3 days 27oc	100	8	ok	
	DAILY WATER CONSUMPTION				
	A) Domestic cu. Mtr/ day	60	25.13	ok	
The water (prevention & control of pollution) act 1974	B) Industrial process cu. Mtr/day	120	10.67	ok	
	c) Industrial cooling cu. Mtr/day	37	1.54	ok	

35. INTERNAL AUDIT (9.2)

Internal audit: Inspection and Verification of effectiveness of system.

Internal audits:

- Technical audits, process audits, and product/service audits.
- Channelize, synchronize and regularize the activity/operations.

The auditsystem involves:

- Audit criterion.
- Audit frequency.
- Audit methodology.

- Auditors qualification and experience.
- Audit plan.
- Auditing procedure.
- Audit reporting.
- Audit compliances and the documents related to it.

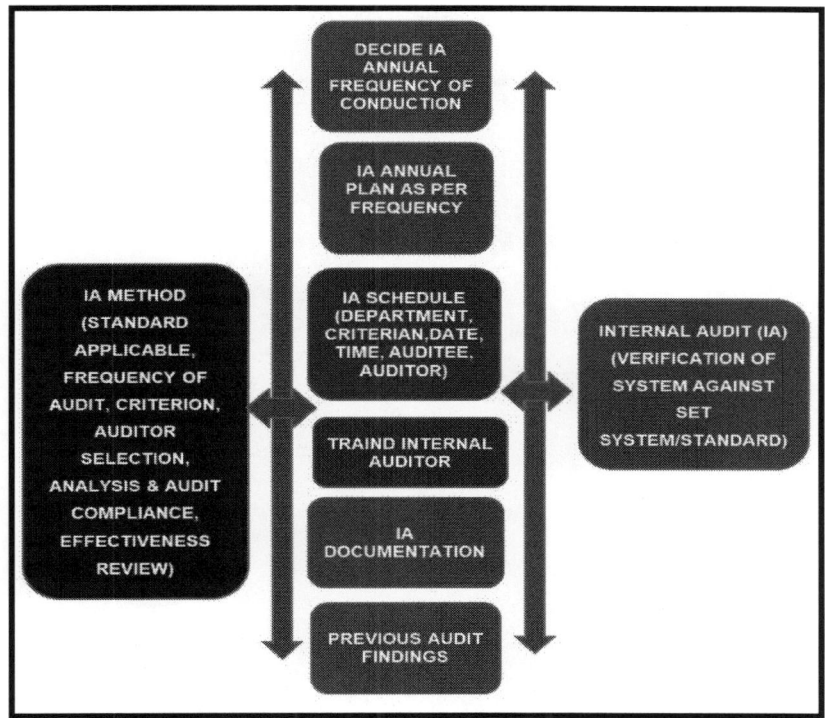

Internal audit

36. AUDIT PROCESS

Guidelines for conduction of internal audit:

1. Form an ISO audit team.
2. Train the team for ISO 14001:2015 internal audits.
3. Prepare internal audit procedure along with internal audit formats.
4. Decide the frequency of audit and prepare the plan for annual internal audit covering all the department/functions along with the top management.

5. Prepare the schedule of internal audit and circulate it at least one week before.

6. Conduct the audit as per schedule.

7. Comply all the audit findings (by responsible department).

8. Prepare the statutory report on the audit findings compliance.

9. Discuss the compliance status, including the findings which require further approvals in management review meeting.

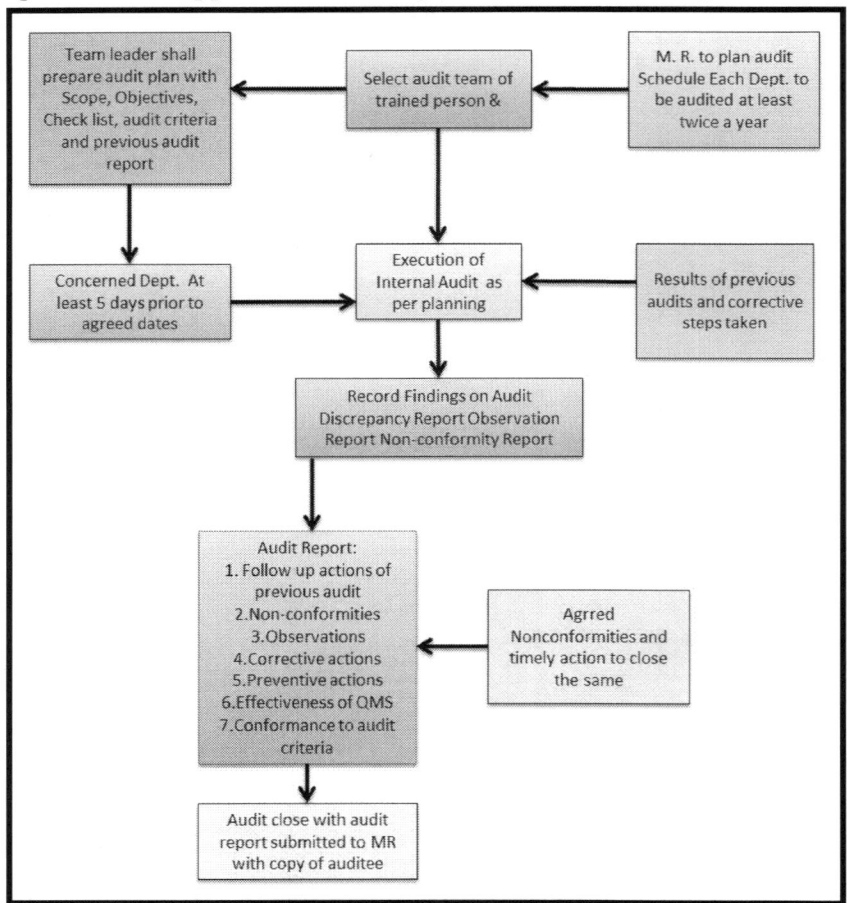

Flow chart of audit process

37. MANAGEMENT REVIEW (9.3)

The agenda of the meeting:

1. Review of Environment policy and Environment objectives for their suitability and effectiveness
2. Results of audits
3. Process performance
4. Status of preventive and corrective actions
5. Follow up actions from previous management review meetings
6. Changes that could affect the Environment management system`
7. Resources requirement
8. Customer complaints and feedback
9. Product performance
10. Compliance to statutory and regulatory requirements.
11. Risk and opportunity management program.
12. Recommendations for Improvement

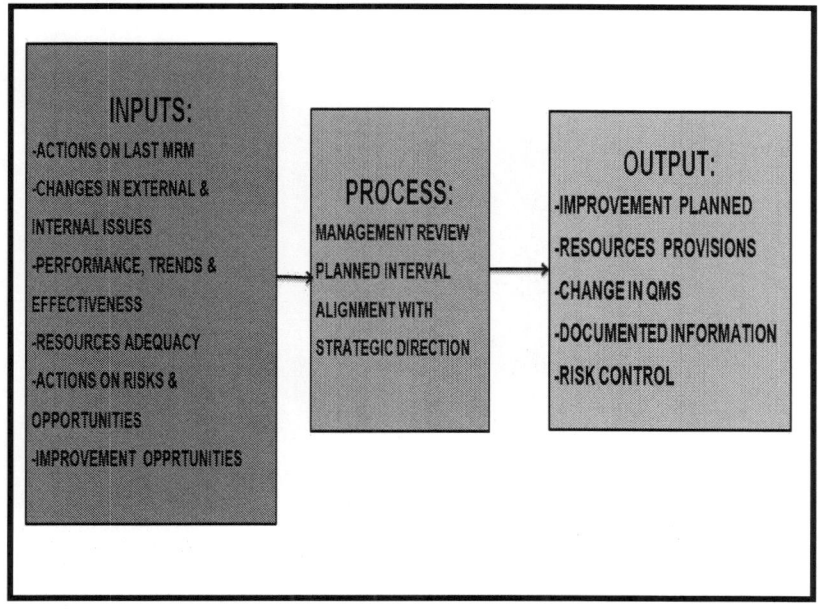

Management review

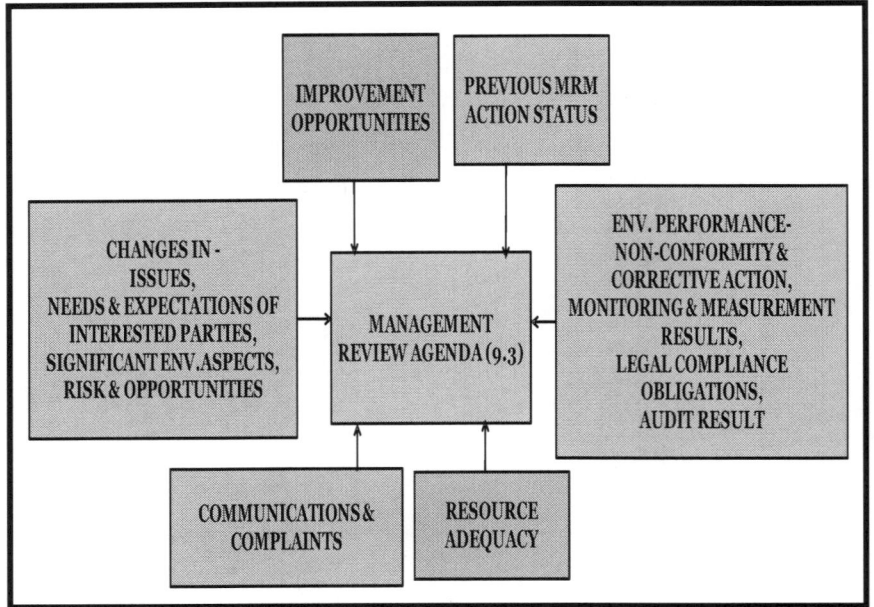

38. IMPROVEMENT (10.0)

The continual improvement process:

➢ Significant breakthrough projects.
➢ Small-step on going improvement activities.

Improvement areas are:

• Results of product, process and EMS audits
• Communications,
• Information systems,
• Processes controls,
• Resources optimization
• Technology

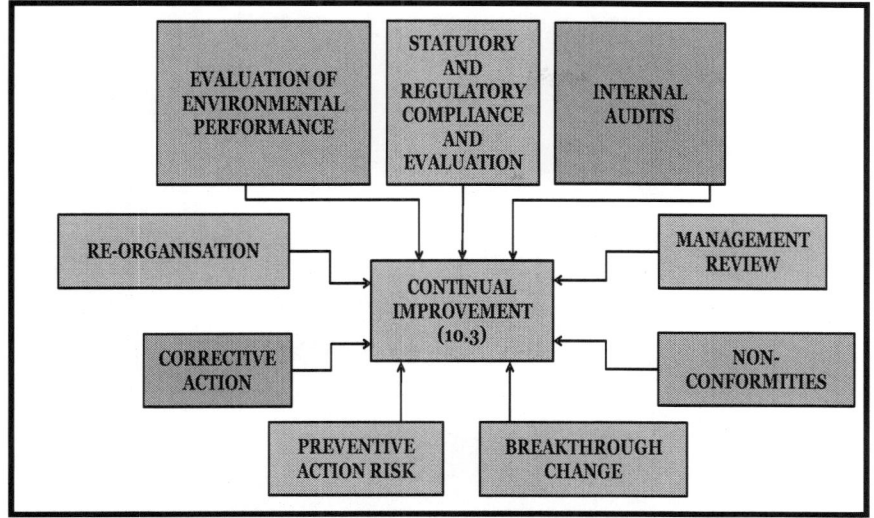

Improvement

39. IMPROVEMENT PROCESS

- Gather information
- Analyse the data and information
- Plan the actions
- Form the team. Assign responsibilities
- Provide resources
- Review periodically
- Assess the improvements

40. NON-CONFIRMITY AND CORRECTIVE ACTIONS

Non- conformity:

- The deviations from the policies, plans, procedures, guidelines, instructions etc.
- The customer feedbacks and complaints
- The feedbacks from interested parties
- Non- compliance to statutory and regulatory compliances.
- Not achieving the targeted goals

- Not implementing the management program
- Identify and detect
- Record and Review.
- Plan Actions
- Control the non -conformity and correct it.
- Deal with the effect of non- conformity in various processes, programs and plans.

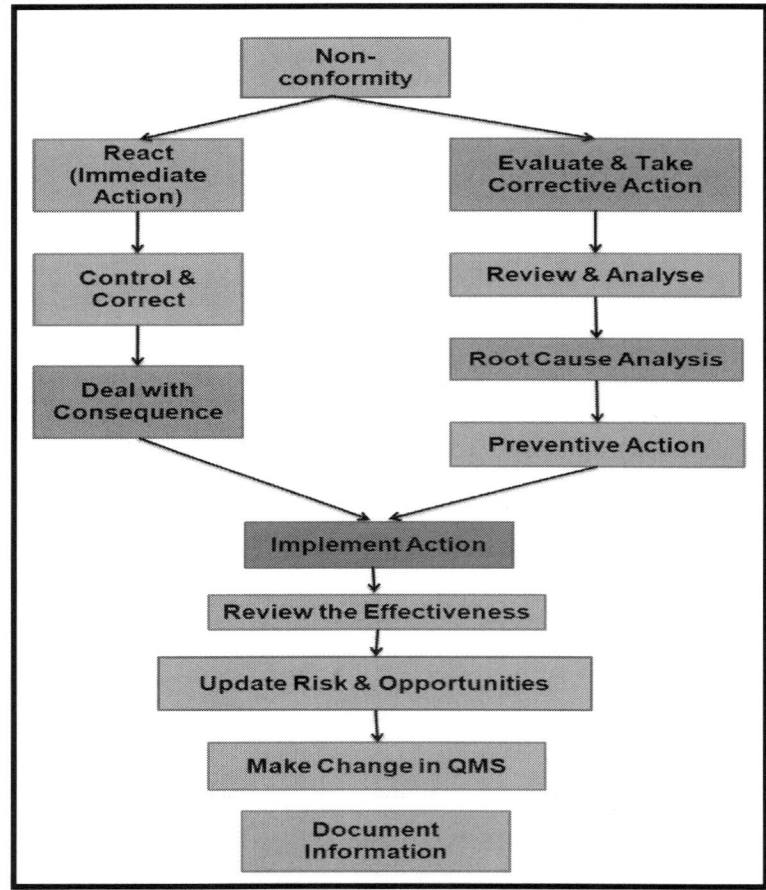

<u>Non-conformity and corrective actions</u>

41. ANALYSIS OF DATA FOR CONTINUAL IMPROVEMENT

The analysis of data related to the process performance:

a) Key performance indicators, objectives, management programmes
b) Customer feedback, complaints, orders and satisfaction surveys
c) Conformity to product specifications, rejections, reworks, acceptance under concession,
d) Characteristics and trends of processes and products
e) Performance of externally provided products, services and processes
f) Breakdown record of machineries and equipment
g) Measurement and monitoring data
Root cause analysis: To eliminate the cause(s) of the nonconformity and to ensure that it does not recur or occur elsewhere.

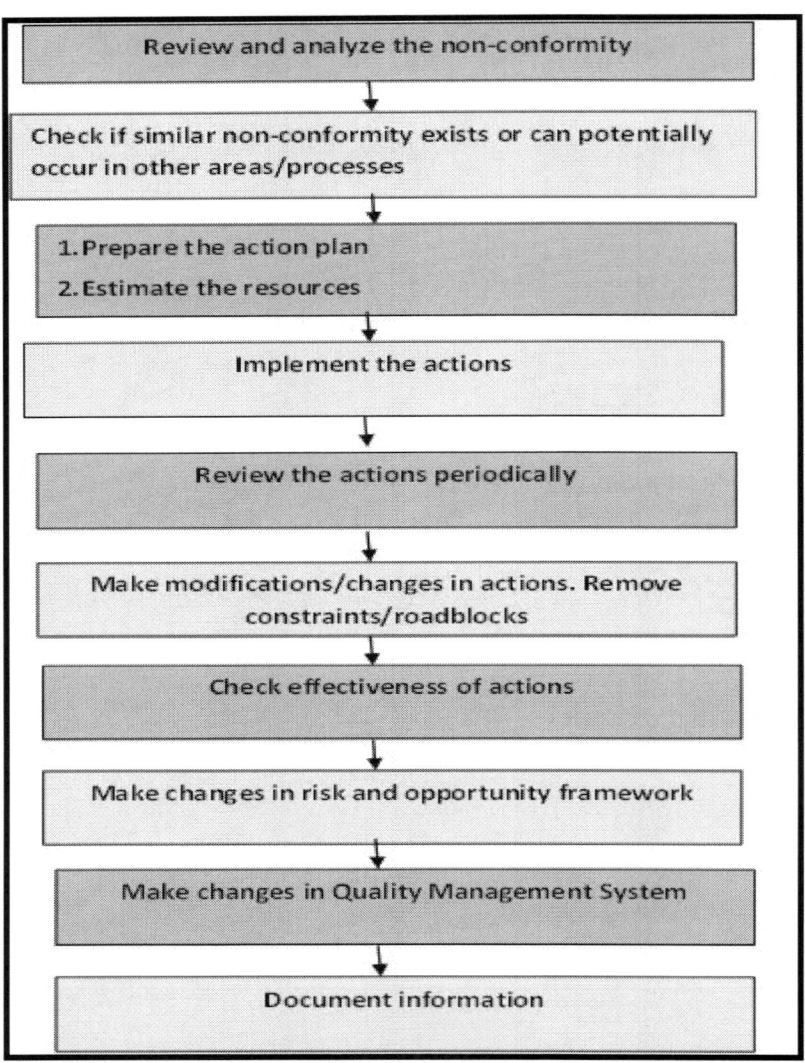

Review and analyze the non-conformity

Check if similar non-conformity exists or can potentially occur in other areas/processes

1. Prepare the action plan
2. Estimate the resources

Implement the actions

Review the actions periodically

Make modifications/changes in actions. Remove constraints/roadblocks

Check effectiveness of actions

Make changes in risk and opportunity framework

Make changes in Quality Management System

Document information

Root cause analysis

42. DOCUMENTATION & IMPLEMENTATION GUIDELINES

1.   Identify & prepare the list of different issues (problems/bottlenecks) facing the organization at functional level and at business level. Issues can be internal (Example- Incompetent staff, inventory management problems) or external (Example-competition).

2.   Identify and prepare the list of applicable interested parties (Stake holders like employee, legal bodies, suppliers, customers etc.), their needs and expectations (Example- clarity about supply, payment matters etc.) , methodology of collection of needs & expectations (Example-Supplier development meeting) , and organization's compliance mechanism system (Example-communication of compliances to interested parties through meetings/emails).

3.   Write the scope of work and boundaries (constraints) of your organization. Boundaries can be physical boundaries.
Also, you can mention the exclusion of sub-clause of clause 8 which may not applicable to you with justification.

4.   Identify and enlist the different functions/processes carried out in your organization. For each process and sub-process, identify the inputs, critical control points (important points/stages of process, risks associated, if not controlled), acceptance criterion, applicable legal, statutory and regulatory requirements, type of controls to be establish to minimize the risk etc.

5.   Prepare the organization chart designation wise and write the roles, responsibilities and authorities for each designation.

6.   Prepare the Environment Policy and objectives to measure and monitor the performance of organization at organization and department level. Set the targets and establish the action plan to achieve these objectives. Objectives should be set for improvement of process and not for monitoring the routine work.

7.   Prepare the risk assessment using different tools like SWOT analysis (Strength, weakness, opportunity & threats) at management

level. For identified weaknesses, opportunities and threats, prepare the action plant to tackle and improve the process.

Prepare the risk assessment table. It includes, identified issues, associated risk for each issue, prioritize the risk and for significant risk, identify and establish the controls. Risk assessment needs to be reviewed periodically to ensure effectiveness of controls established and for newly arisen risks.

8.   Depending on the identified processes, identify the resources required (like, manpower, infrastructure, work environment etc.) and monitor & measure the resources periodically.

1.   Manpower: Prepare the job profile/details designation wise, skill, qualification, experience required and evaluate it. Example - Competency evaluation of staff.

If there is gap between expected and actual, plan and conduct the trainings and knowledge building. Trainings can be through on-job or off-job, through seminars, workshops or knowledge sharing. Maintain the information related to conduction of training. It may be attendance record or photographs.

2.   Infrastructure: Assess and provide the infrastructure for carrying out the work. Infrastructure may be building, laboratory, warehouse, kitchen, machineries, logistics, measuring instruments etc. For maintaining the infrastructure in good condition, prepare and execute preventive maintenance/calibration plan. It also includes provision of safety devices, protective equipment, fire detecting and tackling system, mock-drills, first aid box etc.

3.   Work environment: For carrying out the smooth execution of processes, identify the environmental requirement. For example, temperature, humidity requirements in laboratories, hygiene and infection control required in healthcare units, food industries, ergonomics, air-conditioners required in server rooms. Ensure the environment control.

4.   Communication: Establish the communication ways and modes. Ensure the effectiveness of communication system establish periodically. Here, communication can be through displays, circulars, notices, emails, drawings, photographs etc. Ensure that

communication to be made is understandable i.e. in local language or by symbols as well.

5. Documented Information Control: Identify the documented information (documents, records, displays, drawings, procedures, work instructions, catalogs, forms and formats and legal records: in soft or hard) requirement in your organization. Try to establish the control over it-

1. Give unique identification to documents and records, its issue and revision number, issue and revision date,

2. Decide preparing, reviewing, approving and issuing authority. In soft form, it is by access authorization (for prepare, edit/modify, approve) using password.

3. Establish periodic review system for checking adequacy.

4. Establish document change, updation and distribution system and control. Whenever there requires a change in system (through raising the change request in format or by mail), explore the consequences, interactions in the system. If they are within control then take the approval of concerned authority & make the changes. Revise the Issue /Revision number and date. Mark the 'updated' version as 'Original/master copy' and Issue the current version document to the concerns (at the point of use) marking it with 'controlled copy' with number 1,2... Withdraw the earlier version. Mark that earlier version (if required to retain) by 'obsolete', for soft copy move that file to separate folder. For example, drawing should have clear title, drawing number, Issue/revision number, revision date, approved signature and name etc.

5. Decide the retention period for each documented information considering its functional and legal requirements.

6. Ensure the 'Protection and preservation' of documented information. For example, Hard copy: lamination, bindings, pest controls, Soft copy: Data backup, installing antivirus, saving the data on cloud/google drive, hard disk, password protection, read only format(pdf) etc.

7. Disposal: After retention period, review the documented information, and dispose off the information by weeding out, burning, or by 'Ctrl+delete' command.

9. For core operations of the organization, try to gather interested parties requirements related to product/service. Review the requirements and maintain the record. For any change, because of requirement or because of organizational functional modifications/constraints, communicate it to concern, analyze the consequences, take the approval of authority. Maintain their acceptance and approval record.

10. Identify the risk, emergencies related to process/area which hampers to environment adversely. Prepare the controls to be exercised to avoid and mitigate the emergency impact.

11. Establish the internal audit system:

- Decide Frequency of audit and prepare annual calendar
- Prepare audit schedule (Time-table). Ensure all the departments as declared in scope are covered. Circulate the schedule.
- Train the people: Internal auditor training
- Conduct the audit by trained auditors. Ensure that, auditor can't conduct the audit of self-department.
- Comply the audit findings (by respective responsible department).
- Compile the summery audit findings centrally.

12. Establish Management review system:

- Prepare the Management review team (cross functional: representative from each department).
- Decide the frequency of meetings to be conducted. (Normally gets conducted after internal and external audit)
- Prepare the agenda of meeting and circulate it.
- Conduct the meeting as per agenda.
- Prepare the minutes of meeting along with action plan.
- Circulate the minutes.

13. Establish the Non-conformity and corrective action system:

- Record the non-conformities (process/market performance deviations, output deviations, complaints and feedbacks, safety issues etc.)
- Delegate the responsibility. Can form the team.
- Analyze for its root cause.
- Decide the action: immediate and corrective
- Review and evaluate the effectiveness of action

Maintain the record/information.

14. Improvement:

- Establish the environment amongst the staff to nurture the creativity/innovations. Motivate them.
- Prepare the Environment teams/circles.
- Train the staff: Plan & conduct the talks, presentations, seminars, trainings, expert interactions, industrial visits
- Conduct the competitions, improvement weeks, Kaizen weeks etc.
- Think about: Development and modification projects, Re-engineering projects, Research works, Market analysis
- Prepare and circulate the project learnings (lessons learnt from executed work/project, one point lesson).
- Maintain the record/information.
- Make aware everyone about these improvements.

43. AUTHORS PROFILE

Dr. R. R. LAKHE

Dr. R. R. LAKHE, is presently working as **Director**, Shreyas Quality Management System, SQMS , Nagpur. He is registered Sr. Consultant for ISO9001-2015 QMS and ISO 17025 LQMS with Quality Council of India and is recognized Lean consultant.

He pursues both academic & professional interest. Deeply interested in learning, he has completed, in addition to his PhD in Industrial Engineering, Masters in Management, Sociology, Public Administration, Training& Development. He is Qualified Lead Assessor for ISO9001QMS, ISO14001EMS,ISO 50001ENMS & OHSAS 18001. He is Master Black Belt Six Sigma..

Academically he has guided 14 PhD scholar in both Nagpur &Amaravati University. He is member of RRC in Mumbai University. He is Co-author of Two books; `Handbook of Total Environment Management' & `Total Environment Management for Service Sector' (Published by JAICO Publication). He has to his credit more than 50 papers in International journals of repute and more than 300 papers in National Journal & conferences. He is reviewer for International Journals published by Emerald, Taylor & Francis, Inderscience etc. He is on advisory boards of number of engineering colleges.

Professionally he has provided training & consultancy to more than 200 organisations at national & International level on various performance improvement aspects such as Environment Award, ISO9000, ISO14000, ISO50001 ENMS,OHSAS1 8000, ISO22000,ISO17025, 5 S, Kaizen, Six Sigma, NABL accreditation, FAMI-QS,BIFMA.

He is active member of various professional associations such as Institution of Engineers(I), ISTE, ISTD,IIIE,IES etc and has been organizing conferences on Quality Progress. He is active member of various professional associations such as IE(I), ISTE, IIIE, ISE, ISTD, IIPE, IIMM, NIQR and organizes conferences seminars on Environment every year.

He loves travelling and has travelled to Europe, USA, South-East Asian countries both as a part of business as well as pleasure.

KRANTI DHARKAR

Kranti Dharkar is presently working as **Sr. Consultant** with Shreyas Quality Management System and QCI registered Lean consultant having 12+years of experience. She has done ElectronicsEngineering and MBA (Operations). She is auditor for ISO 9001QMS, ISO14001 EMS, ISO 17025 NABL, ISO 50001& OHSAS 18001/ISO45001. She has also contributed in getting Quality awards like CII SCALE, Ramkrishna Bajaj, Rajiv Gandhi National awards.She has conducted number of training programmes on ISO 9001, ISO 14001, OHSAS18001/ISO45001, ISO 27001 ISMS, 5S, Lean, Six Sigma, SPC, MSA, ISO/TS 16949 etc. and has also provided consultancy in these areas. She has conducted ISO audits, provided consultancy and training to various organizations from diverse sectors such as Thermal power Station, Pharmaceutical industries, Logistic management, Automobile andFurniture industries, Hazardous waste industries, Software industries, Healthcare services, Engineering services etc.

Milind Joshi

Director
Surya Envirotech

B. Tech (Chemical Engineering), M. Tech (Chemical Engineering), Chartered Chemical Engineer, Advance Post Graduate Diploma in Industrial Safety, M. S.W. (Community Development)

Certified Lead Auditor for ISO 50001:2013 (Energy Management System),ISO 45001-2018 (Occupational Health & Safety Management System),ISO 14001-2015 (Environment Management System), ISO 9001-2015 (Quality Management System)

Mr.Milind Joshi holds more than 20 years extensive experience in Environmental conservation and occupational Health & Safety in process industries

Mr.Milind Joshi has provided consultancy to more than 200 organization from manufacturing and process industries. He has conducted trainings on Industrial Safety and Environmental Conservation for sustainable Development. He is active member of various professional associations such as VigyanBharti, Institution of Engineers.

Manufactured by Amazon.ca
Bolton, ON

31670860R00030